DIESELS AND ELECTRICS IN LONDON AND THE SOUTH EAST

MALCOLM BATTEN

AMBERLEY

First published 2019

Amberley Publishing
The Hill, Stroud
Gloucestershire, GL5 4EP

www.amberley-books.com

Copyright © Malcolm Batten, 2019

The right of Malcolm Batten to be identified
as the Author of this work has been asserted in
accordance with the Copyrights, Designs and
Patents Act 1988.

ISBN 978 1 4456 9057 5 (print)
ISBN 978 1 4456 9058 2 (ebook)

British Library Cataloguing in Publication Data.
A catalogue record for this book is available from
the British Library.

Typesetting by Aura Technology and Software
Services, India. Printed in the UK.

Introduction

The railway lines of London and the South East include tracks from all four of the constituent companies that made up British Railways and subsequently became the Eastern, Midland, Southern and Western Regions. Each region took a separate approach when diesels and electrics replaced steam in the 1950s–60s. Consequently particular classes of 'first generation' diesel and electric locomotives became associated with specific regions, or even areas within a region, and were rarely seen elsewhere. The Western Region alone opted for diesel-hydraulic transmission, as adopted in Germany, whereas the other regions chose diesel-electrics. These would be culled in the 1970s as non-standard and replaced by diesel-electrics drafted in from the other regions. The Southern Region had extensive third rail electrification and developed both electric locomotives (Class 71) and bi-mode electro-diesel locomotives (Class 73). They also opted for diesel-electric rather than diesel-mechanical DMUs, although these are outside the scope of this book.

In June 1986 Network SouthEast was launched to collectively market passenger services throughout this area, with a distinctive livery applied to locomotives, rolling stock and stations. Although NSE-liveried locos were not intended to be used on freight work, they might appear on maintenance trains for instance, as well as passenger traffic.

The years 1986–88 saw a livery explosion when British Rail was divided into business sectors rather than geographical regions. Locomotives received different liveries according to the sector work they were allocated to: Inter-City, Provincial, Parcels, and Railfreight, which applied separate decals for Construction, Petroleum, Distribution and Coal traffic-allocated pools.

In preparation for privatisation, in 1994 Railfreight was split into three geographical operating companies: Mainline, Loadhaul, and Transrail. There was also Railfreight Distribution, Rail Express Systems (for parcels and mail trains) and Freightliner. Each had their own liveries. There were also a number of 'one-off', historic and special liveries at this time. The stone traffic from the Mendips quarries saw the first use of foreign-built and privately owned diesel classes when the General Motors Class 59/0 and 59/1 locos were introduced by Foster Yeoman in 1986, and then by ARC Ltd in 1990. These now operate collectively under the Mendip Rail name.

Privatisation from 1995–6 saw the remaining first generation diesel locomotives and multiple units pass to several new owners and train operating companies, with each applying their own livery. The former Railfreight companies and Railfreight Distribution were bought by Wisconsin Railways, trading as English Welsh & Scottish Railway (EWS). The other main freight haulier was Freightliner. EWS would later pass to Deutsche Bahn in 2007, renamed DB Schenker in 2009, while other new companies have come and gone. Those that have stayed the course into 2018 include GB Rail Freight (GBRF), Direct Rail Services (DRS) and Colas Rail.

Locomotive haulage of passenger trains was once the norm. Coaches were removed to and from carriage sidings as empty stock for servicing. The introduction of the HST in the 1970s, electrification and DMUs have replaced loco haulage in most cases. Where loco haulage remains the trains stay in fixed formation working in push-pull mode with a driving trailer. This persists at the time of writing on the LNER (King's Cross) with Class 91s, Greater Anglia (Liverpool Street) with Class 90s, and the Chiltern Line (Marylebone) with Class 68s. Servicing (replenishing water tanks, restocking buffets where applicable, etc.) takes place at terminal stations.

The most common situation now where locomotives can be found hauling passenger trains that are not in push-pull mode is with charter specials. These may be enthusiast tours with steam, diesel or electric haulage and their associated empty stock workings, 'Footex' and similar excursions, or luxury trips using the Belmond British Pullman or Northern Belle coaching stock. Specialist companies such as West Coast Railways provide the locomotives, crews and stock for many of these special trains.

This book features a selection of diesel and electric locomotives in an area of some 50–60 miles from the capital since 1969. It takes the form of visiting the lines from each of the main London termini, plus the main connecting lines, showing a typical selection of the freight and passenger workings to be seen on each route.

Photographers should note that not all the locations featured in this book remain suitable for use today. Some lines have since been electrified, footbridges have been meshed in, replaced or just removed, and on some main lines out of London, such as the Great Eastern and Great Western, the main line tracks have been fenced off from the suburban lines to prevent would-be suicides. A laudable cause no doubt, but a nuisance for photographers. These instances will be noted in the captions.

All photographs are by the author except where credited.

Flashback

How it all began! The only main line passenger diesel locomotive inherited by British Railways in 1948 was No. 10000, completed by the LMS in 1947. It is seen here on the Midland Main Line from St Pancras at Elstree in 1948. In that year it would be joined by similar loco No. 10001. Both locomotives continued into the 1960s, but sadly neither was considered for preservation despite their historic significance. (*Reg Batten*)

The first regular allocation of diesels on passenger work came in 1958, when the first of the English Electric Type 4 (later Class 40) 1 Co-Co 1 locomotives were allocated to Stratford for Liverpool Street–Norwich services along the former Great Eastern Railway route, replacing Britannia steam locos. This example is passing Romford on a journey to London when nearly new. Note the lack of a yellow warning panel on the front – these did not appear until the 1960s. (*Reg Batten*)

After the success of the prototype, twenty-two English Electric 'Deltic' 3300bhp locomotives were bought for principal services on the East Coast Main Line. These entered service in 1961 and remained on these duties until replacement by HSTs, being withdrawn in 1981. This example in original green livery was seen at Potters Bar in 1968. (*Reg Batten*)

The London end of the East Coast Main Line sees little freight traffic now, but saw far more in the 1960s and 1970s. Here an unidentifiable Class 40 heads a vans train including several four-wheel wagons along the slow line near Potters Bar in the mid-1960s. (*Reg Batten*)

The electrification of the West Coast Main Line was the major project of the 1960s. Electric traction reached the rebuilt Euston station in 1966 and a pair of AL6 (later Class 86) locos are seen at the heads of trains waiting to depart for the north in 1968. (*Reg Batten*)

The Western Region hydraulic era is typified by this picture of Beyer Peacock Hymek D7026 at Oxford station before the station buildings were rebuilt. The last of these were withdrawn in 1975. (*Reg Batten*)

Class 47s took over from Class 40s on the London–Norwich services and remained until electrification was completed throughout in 1985–7. Class 86s took over as far as Ipswich from 13 May 1985. This busy scene at Liverpool Street station on 17 May 1985 shows No. 86244 *The Royal British Legion* awaiting departure as another of the class moves out, released by the departure of the train it had brought in. A Class 47 can also be seen with a train for King's Lynn.

In InterCity livery, No. 86247 *Abraham Darby* passes through a snowy Stratford near the end of its journey. 8 February 1986.

Network SouthEast was launched at Liverpool Street station on 9 June 1986 when Class 47 No. 47573 was named *The London Standard*. Here it is awaiting the formal unveiling of its name.

The Class 47s continued to work trains to King's Lynn and here No. 47585 *County of Cambridgeshire* passes through Hackney Downs on a train to the capital on 8 August 1987. The white roof was a Stratford characteristic.

On 6 July 1989, a then nearly new Class 90 passes the signal box at Stratford station with a test train attracting the keen interest of the signal box staff. This may have been to test clearances prior to the class being passed for use on the GE lines. A pair of Southend line EMUs provide a load. Little did we know that the Class 90s would later become the regular motive power for London–Norwich trains.

Privatisation and changes of train operating companies has seen a variety of liveries on East Anglia services since the 1990s. No. 86227 stands in Liverpool Street on 12 August 2002 in Anglia franchise livery. Note the Union Jack – 2002 was the Golden Jubilee of HM the Queen's reign.

Stratford again in May 2006 and now the operator is the ridiculously named 'One' (as in 'the 1.30 One service'). Class 90s have replaced the Class 86s and No. 90015 is at the head of this train.

The current operator in 2019 is Greater Anglia, and their livery is seen on No. 90003 entering Colchester with a train for London. The Class 90s remain attached to the London end of the trains, with a driving trailer at the country end.

Crossing the river at Manningtree on 14 June 2017 is No. 90015 *Colchester Castle* on one of the regular half-hourly Norwich–London trains.

In the 1960s, Stratford still had a requirement for small short-wheelbase shunters to shunt the London docks. But the docks closed down between 1968 and 1983 and so the requirement ended. A pair of Drewry shunters can be seen on shed in 1969 with D2223 in the foreground.

Also a local feature of Stratford at this time were the British Thompson Houston and North British Type 1 diesels (Classes 15 and 16). Examples of both classes are seen in 1969 but the unreliable North British locomotives would be withdrawn that year. Meanwhile, the Class 15s were already on their way out.

Stratford depot's Class 08 shunter No. 08833 (formerly D4001) was used as the Liverpool Street station pilot and received this special livery. It features an early BR lion and wheel totem and the Stratford 'Cockney sparrow' emblem. It was on duty at the terminus during rebuilding work on 15 March 1987.

Coming off the North London Line and passing through Stratford on 25 September 2002, Direct Rail Services Class 20s Nos 20312 and 20311 haul a nuclear flask working for Bradwell Power Station. This will take them to Southminster, at the end of the single line from Wickford. The train ran only as required, but because the line is single track with only one passing loop, a gap had to be left in the passenger service one day a week to create a path for the train.

Freightliner traffic to and from Felixstowe docks is the major freight traffic on the Great Eastern lines. On 3 August 1989 a train for Felixstowe passes Manor Park headed by Class 37s Nos 37095 and 37116.

With electrification of the North London Line, these Freightliner trains can now be electrically hauled around London and as far east as Ipswich. However, many retain diesel haulage and here Freightliner Class 66 No. 66592 *Johnson Stevens Agencies* works a westbound train at Manningtree on 14 June 2017.

An open day at Ilford Car Sheds on 20 May 1989 saw the unique Class 89 electric locomotive among the many exhibits on show.

The stabling point at Colchester would usually house a number of locomotives and was readily visible from the long London-bound platform. On 24 October 1987 a pair of Class 37s and resident Class 03 No. 03059 are conveniently located for the photographer.

Another open day at Colchester TMD on 2 May 1988 had seen resident Class 08 shunter No. 08772 repainted BR green and named *Camulodunum* (the Roman name for Colchester).

As previously mentioned, English Electric Type 4s pioneered passenger diesel work on the Great Eastern lines. The doyen of the Class, D200 (later No. 40122), was preserved by the National Railway Museum and used for several specials before retirement from main line work. On 16 April 1988 it made a final run over the Liverpool Street–Norwich route. It was photographed passing Manor Park in less than ideal weather conditions! The headboard was a reprise of that fitted on the locomotive's first run over the route on 16 April 1958.

Most suburban branches only see locomotives traversing them when there is track maintenance or on the occasional enthusiasts' special. It was the latter that led to the unusual sight of a DRS Class 20 on the Chingford line on 26 January 2013. No. 20312 is heading the Pathfinder tour as it approaches Highams Park station on the return leg of this part of the tour. A DRS Class 37, No. 37409 *Lord Hinton*, was on the rear. A second Class 20 was also used on this tour but had been left in Liverpool Street during this stage.

Engineering work has closed the west side of Liverpool Street station on 24 May 2003. GBRF Class 66 No. 66704 *Colchester Power Signalbox* is on hand while similar No. 66003 of rival EWS can be seen in the shadows beyond.

London, Tilbury & Southend/C2C line from Fenchurch Street

Locomotive-hauled passenger trains are a rarity on this line – the only examples tend to be enthusiast specials, and West Coast Railways No. 37416 is indeed on a Pathfinder Tours excursion. The location is Limehouse and the date 19 February 2005.

Barking–Gospel Oak line

The Barking–Gospel Oak radial route remains an important freight route, allowing traffic to and from the Tilbury area to bypass Stratford. On 24 October 1985 No. 47291 arrives at Gospel Oak, from where it will proceed onto the North London Line towards Willesden Junction. Some wag has enhanced (?) the front of the locomotive with a 'Thomas' face.

Passenger services are normally worked by DMUs, but in 1999 rolling stock shortages led to the temporary hire of a Class 33/1 and former Southern Region 3TC set. No. 33103 was seen at Upper Holloway on 24 August. Passenger services were proposed for withdrawal under the Beeching cuts, but subsequent investment and the inclusion of the line in the TfL-run London Overground has vastly increased the traffic. The line has now been electrified and electric passenger services began in early 2019.

Class 31 No. 31163 approaches Homerton with a nuclear flask train for Southminster on 26 September 1996. Note the line has third rail electrification for the passenger service from North Woolwich to Richmond, then worked by ex-Southern Region 2EPB units. There is also overhead AC electrification from Camden Road for through freight traffic from the West Coast Main Line to the Great Eastern Line.

In November 1987 the line had not been overhead electrified throughout. This is Homerton again. The train is the 07.50 Harwich Parkeston Quay–Glasgow/Edinburgh, routed via the North London Line, for which a diesel drag was provided. No. 47433 hauls No. 86222 *Lloyd's List*.

On 28 May 2011 a pair of Class 31s work an enthusiast railtour at Brondesbury. Note that the third rail has now been removed. The passenger service is now worked by London Overground.

With the electrification of the Barking–Gospel Oak line in 2018, electrically hauled through freights to the Tilbury line are now possible. The only service so booked in autumn 2018 was the Dagenham–Mossend Ford cars train and return empties. DBS Class 90 No. 90135 comes off the Kensal Green chord to join the West Coast Main Line on 26 September.

Loco-hauled passenger trains on the ECML are worked by Class 91 electrics. These are normally at the north end of the train with a driving trailer at the London end. This Class 91, seen in 1997 at King's Cross in GNER livery, unusually has the blunt end leading.

Well into its stride as it passes Biggleswade, a Class 91 in GNER colours heads north on 14 September 2003.

The ECML franchise has undergone a number of changes including twice being taken back under state control. In Virgin livery, No. 91114 *Durham Cathedral* leans to the curve as it heads north through Harringay on 29 April 2017.

The unique Class 89 locomotive was in service at King's Cross on 14 August 1997. It now carried GNER livery in contrast to the earlier view in 1989. See page 15.

The ECML main line passenger trains are maintained at Bounds Green depot near Alexandra Palace station. In November 1985 when this picture was taken, it was Mark 1 stock and Class 47s being serviced with No. 08930 in attendance. The stock has changed but Class 08s are still used as shed pilots here in 2019.

Until 8 November 1976 when electric services took over the local workings to Welwyn Garden City and Stevenage, Class 31s worked trains of suburban compartment stock on peak-hour trains to Moorgate. These traversed the 'Widened lines', accessed via the King's Cross York Road platform. Here No. 31173 approaches Farringdon with a service to Moorgate during the last week. The Underground tracks are to the right behind the railings. The GN electric services now operate via Drayton Park on the Northern City route to Moorgate, which was previously run as part of the Underground Northern Line.

No. 47481 *Sunstar* stands in King's Cross Platform 1 with a parcels train on 31 August 1993.

Strangers in the camp! Class 33s No. 33116/D6535 *Hertfordshire Railtours* and No. 33051 prepare to work the 'Swineshead Revisted' railtour on 22 March 1997. This ran to Skegness via Nottingham and the then newly reopened line through Mansfield to Worksop.

Another railtour sees two Class 37s newly repainted in EWS livery, Nos 37051 *Merehead* and 37057 *Viking*. They are approaching Stevenage on 20 July 1996.

The Class 31s had a long association with the ECML, including working both passenger and freight trains, as well as suburban trains to London Moorgate and Cambridge line trains. No. 31434 was at Peterborough, then not electrified, on 13 September 1986.

Midland Main Line from St Pancras

The Peaks had a long association with the Midland Main Line, working most passenger trains until displaced by HSTs. No. 45128 waits at St Pancras with an evening parcels train on 8 May 1986.

It is 17.38 p.m. at St Pancras, but it is mail and parcels traffic that fills the platforms, not commuters, so it is presumably a weekend. No. 47587 has probably been transferred from the Network SouthEast pool to the RES pool and is showing evidence of having lost its name, *Ruskin College Oxford* (but not livery), in the process. 21 May 1993.

We saw D200/No. 40122 before, working a tour from Liverpool Street. Here it prepares to work 'The Corby Cutler' from St Pancras on 4 May 1987.

The Bedford–Bletchley local service is normally a DMU operation but shortages in 1998 led to the service being worked by a pair of Fragonset Class 31s top-and-tailing a pair of coaches. Nos 31468 and 31452 are pictured entering Stewartby on 18 October.

On 6 April 1999, No. 37717 *Berwick Middle School* was seen near Millbrook on the Bedford–Bletchley line with an engineering works train.

West Coast Main Line from Euston

Two main line passenger trains stop at Watford Junction on 17 October 1989. The London-bound train is hauled by No. 86234 *J.B. Priestly O.M.* in InterCity livery.

Virgin have held the franchise for WCML inter-city trains since privatisation. Class 87 No. 87008 hauls a train in matching Virgin livery northwards at Headstone Lane on 9 May 2000.

By contrast No. 87028 *Lord President* retains InterCity livery while the carriages all carry Virgin colours. It is passing North Wembley on 1 July 1998.

Class 86 No. 86233 was given a repaint in original style electric blue livery in 2002 and is seen passing North Wembley on 4 July 2003. The coaches are in Virgin livery.

Class 90s were also used until the current Pendolino trains displaced them. No. 90002 *Mission Impossible* passes Carpenders Park on 8 April 1997

The only regular loco-hauled passenger service on the WCML now are the overnight Caledonian Sleeper services. No. 87002 *Royal Sovereign* brings the empty stock from an overnight Caledonian Sleeper service through Willesden Junction to the carriage sidings at Stonebridge Park on 3 November 2018.

At Carpenders Park, Class 92 No. 92042 *Honegger* works an intermodal freight northwards on 10 May 2001.

Heading south at Carpenders Park on 25 March 2003 was No. 47757 *Capability Brown*, one of the few of this class to receive EWS livery. It is working a Serco test train, which is being tailed by another Class 47.

Chiltern Line from Marylebone

Regular loco-hauled passenger trains returned to the Chiltern lines for the first time since 1966 when the Wrexham & Shropshire open access operation started in April 2008. Class 67s top-and-tailed the trains. No. 67013 is the lead locomotive on this train at Neasden on 10 May 2008.

Other locomotives used retained EWS livery, such as No. 67028, seen heading a northbound train at Neasden on 1 June 2008.

The Wrexham & Shropshire services ceased in January 2011 after a review concluded there was no prospect of the business ever being profitable, but the locomotives and stock passed to Chiltern Railways for use to Birmingham. No. 67013 is on the rear end of a train entering High Wycombe on 24 March 2015.

The Class 67s were replaced by new Class 68s in 2015. No. 68010 works an evening peak hour train for Birmingham at Neasden on 30 June 2015.

While some of the Class 68s carry Chiltern Railways livery, others are in Direct Rail Services colours such as No. 68009 *Titan* at Marylebone on 23 June 2018. The 68s are at country end of the trains – driving trailers are now used at the London end.

Something a little different! Preserved Western D1015 *Western Champion* and Tyseley-based Class 47 D1755 double-head a returning special train at Neasden on 9 February 2014.

Seen stabled in the sidings at Neasden on 30 January 1994 was No. 20169, painted in Balfour Beatty livery.

EWS Class No. 66154 works a 'Binliner' train of containerised domestic waste for landfill through the cutting north of High Wycombe station on 24 March 2015.

EWS Class 66 No. 66030 heads a 'Binliner' train for the landfill site at Calvert through Quainton Road, north of Aylesbury, on 17 October 1999. The freight-only line beyond Aylesbury Vale Parkway bisects the site of the Buckinghamshire Steam Centre at Quainton Road.

The start of Great Western journeys is at Paddington. The Class 50s had originally been built to replace Class 40s on the West Coast Main Line between Crewe and Glasgow, but when that line was electrified they were cascaded to the Western Region. No. 50009 *Conqueror* awaits departure on 24 April 1986.

On 22 June 2002 Virgin Class 47 No. 47806 awaits departure from Platform 1. This was probably a diverted service to Birmingham because of engineering works on the WCML.

Loco-hauled passenger services at Paddington are now restricted to the overnight sleeper service for which First Great Western uses Class 57s. No. 57604 *Pendennis Castle*, in traditional GWR livery, stands at the buffers with the stock on 18 October 2014.

Back in 1969, diesel-hydraulics were still the mainstay of Western Region services. These North British-built Class 22s, such as D6328, were utilised on empty stock workings between Old Oak Common and Paddington – a role previously held by steam 0-6-0PT pannier tanks.

The seventy-four Class 52 Westerns and seventy-one Class 42 and 43 Warships were the principal power for express trains and examples of both can be seen here on shed. These could be found in a variety of liveries including green or maroon, or as here on D1055 *Western Advocate*, BR blue. Like the previous picture this is taken at Old Oak Common depot. The last Westerns went in 1976.

Although the diesel-hydraulics went quite early, examples of Hymeks, Warships and Westerns have all been preserved. Here, a representative selection of the types were on show at an open day held at Old Oak Common depot on 4 August 2000.

Class 50 No. 50011, then unnamed, stands on one of the roads leading off from the turntable at Old Oak Common depot on 26 May 1975.

Several of the Class 50s have passed into preservation after their relatively short service life, and five examples can be seen here at the Old Oak Common depot open day, held on 2 September 2017.

Old Oak Common was another London depot that employed Class 08 shunters as depot pilots. At the 2017 open day, No. 08483 *Neil* was looking resplendent in a coat of early BR black with the original lion and wheel emblem.

Examples of the Class 57s used on the night sleeper train were also on display. No. 57603 *Tintagel Castle* in the latest GWR livery was exhibited in the maintenance shop.

The Western Region had a batch of five diesel shunters intended solely for departmental use and numbered in a separate series. No. 97654 (formerly PWM654) was working at Paddington during rebuilding work to simplify the approach tracks to the station on 10 April 1993.

The Great Western line is one of the busiest in London for freight traffic, even into 2019. Back in May 1995, before electrification to Heathrow spoilt the view, Class 60 No. 60078 *Stac Pollaidh* approaches Ealing Broadway.

Looking the other way from the bridge seen in the distance in the previous picture, Hunslet Barclay-liveried Class 20 No. 20904 *Janis* is on the rear of a weedkilling train, headed by a sister locomotive. 16 August 1990.

Before electrification, the footbridge known locally as 'Jacob's Ladder' at West Ealing was a popular location for photographers. Peak No. 45051 is passing with a train of coaches from the research department based at Derby. 20 November 1986.

West Ealing is the junction for the Greenford loop. At Castle Bar Park on this line, a pair of Class 37s, Nos 37889 and 37717, work an empty aggregates train which has unloaded at the terminal at Park Royal. A two-car Class 165 DMU pauses in the station with a service for Greenford. 8 April 1998.

The next stop on the line is South Greenford and here a pair of Class 33s, Nos 33040 and 33053, head north with another aggregates train on 13 September 1990. This train will probably have originated at Angerstein Wharf near Charlton.

Passing the Central Line station at Hanger Lane is No. 47650 on the GW line to West Ruislip and High Wycombe, which these days sees very little use. The date is 8 May 1989. The cabling beside the Central Line has been raised considerably now, so this view is no longer feasible.

With semaphore signalling much in evidence, No. 50024 *Vanguard* speeds through South Ruislip on 15 June 1989. This is probably the 17.40 Paddington–Wolverhampton, which was the last surviving loco-hauled service routed this way via High Wycombe. Both locomotive and stock are in Network SouthEast livery.

Back on the main line to Reading and there is snow on the tracks at West Drayton as No. 47812 heads for the capital on 20 February 1986.

Sporting Great Western franchise livery, Class 47 No. 47815 is seen near Iver with a rake of Mark 1 charter coaches on 16 March 1999. This was probably a special train run in connection with the Cheltenham Race Meeting.

Coming the other way on the same day, EWS-liveried No. 37718 hauls Underground Tube stock back from overhaul. The barrier wagons are 'translator' wagons as the couplings on the tube stock will not be compatible with those on the loco.

Passing through Platform 6 at Slough on 4 August 1998, No. 56080 *Selby Coalfield* has charge of a train of oil tankers. This was probably destined for the oil terminal at Langley – the next station towards London.

Passing the Slough Trading Estate, to the west of the station, is EWS No. 66106 with empty steel carrier wagons. 8 June 2000.

Freightliner's No. 66601 *The Hope Valley* approaches Taplow with an eastbound train. 2 September 2010.

Super power for a super-long train! One of the Mendip Rail 'Jumbo' trains passes through Maidenhead station headed by EWS Class 59/2 No. 59205 and Mendip Rail Class 59/1 No. 59104 *Village of Great Elm*. The date is 3 September 2010.

The GWR main line passes through a cutting at Ruscombe on the approach to Twyford. Freightliner's No. 66623 *Bill Bolsover* in Bardon Aggregates blue livery works a Theale–Earles empty cement tank train eastwards on 10 March 2015. The wide spacing of the tracks can be traced back to the railway's origins as a broad gauge route.

About to pass through Twyford station, Mendip Rail No. 59102 *Village of Chantry* working empty wagons back to the quarries is overtaken by a Class 165 DMU on the fast line. 27 May 2015.

Much has changed since this photo of No. 31447 on a parcels train at Reading was taken in 1986, including the complete rebuilding of the station.

The next station west of Reading is Tilehurst. Approaching the station on 12 June 2014 is Freightliner No. 66572 on one of the many container trains that pass through here. This was taken from the new footbridge now installed.

Tilehurst station still retained much of its Great Western character when EWS No. 66111 passed through with covered car carriers on 24 July 2013. Since then, electrification and replacement of the footbridge by an accessible one have altered the appearance substantially.

A footbridge just to the west of the station used to offer excellent opportunities before the wires went up. Colas Class 56 No. 56113 powers the Tilbury–Llanwern steel empties on 30 July 2014.

The view in the opposite direction featured sweeping curves and trees, behind which flows the River Thames. Freightliner trains are a frequent sight here, working south to Southampton Docks, for which they will turn off towards Basingstoke at Reading West Junction. No. 70011 does the honours on 30 July 2014.

Sweeping curves and a deep cutting are the pattern as the line continues through Purley-on-Thames. A DBS Class 60 was usually rostered for 13.35 Theale–Robeston empty Murco tanks and No. 60019 was the locomotive on 12 June 2014.

Coming the other way – yet another Freightliner train with No. 66502 on the helm seen on the same day.

Passing through Goring & Streatley station is an earlier example of Freightliner power, namely No. 57001 *Freightliner Pioneer*, on 13 June 2000. The road bridge here was later replaced, its successor having a much higher parapet.

A bridge to the west of Cholsey & Moulsford station was another location popular with photographers. The colourful 13.35 Theale–Robeston empty Murco tanks train was routed down the fast line behind Loadhaul-liveried No. 60059 *Swinden Dalesman* on this occasion – 23 April 2002.

Approaching Didcot from the east are Nos 37519 and 37673 with a train of open bogie wagons. 25 June 1999.

Didcot is the junction for Oxford and the north, and also has a goods yard. Locomotives can usually be found stabled here between duties. On 29 May 1989 No. 37235 *The Coal Merchants Association of Scotland* is seen with another of the class and a Class 08 shunter. The cooling towers and chimney of the power station form the backdrop.

On 8 June 2014 a pair of DRS Class 37s, No. 37610 *T.S. (Ted) Cassady 14.5.61–6.4.08* and No. 37607, were stabled with the Network Rail inspection train.

A period scene from Didcot in 1986 as GWR-liveried No. 47484 *Isambard Kingdom Brunel* departs towards Oxford. Note the mineral wagons in the sidings and coaches from the Great Western Society, whose steam centre occupies the former loco shed site.

Taking the direct route towards Swindon, a pair of Colas Class 56s head the Tilbury–Llanwern steel empties on 16 August 2014. No. 56113 is again in use as the lead locomotive.

At Didcot North Junction, Freightliner No. 66558 has arrived by the station avoiding line, which skirts the Didcot Steam Centre. The middle pair of tracks are those from the station, on which we previously saw No. 47484 departing. The right-hand tracks come from the Swindon line via Foxhall Junction.

No. 66569 sweeps southwards, and will take the station avoiding line towards Reading and eventually to Southampton. Both pictures were taken on 5 September 2013.

The line to Oxford passes through the local stations of Appleford and Culham. On 7 April 1990 No. 47587 passes through Appleford, which still retained wooden platforms and GWR pagoda-style waiting shelters.

Passing through the next station at Radley is Network SouthEast-liveried No. 47716 *Duke of Edinburgh's Award*, which had previously been based on the Scottish Region and fitted for Glasgow–Edinburgh push-pull working. London to Oxford fast trains came under the NSE aegis and were worked by either Class 47s or Class 50s at this time. 13 July 1990.

NSE Class 47s were not the only examples of their type on passenger work through Oxford, as Virgin CrossCountry also employed them on their services. No. 48817 works a typical train as it passes Hinksey Yard, south of Oxford.

In 1988, Didcot Power Station was still operational and receiving coal from the north via Oxford. No. 58034 passes Hinksey Yard with another consignment on 17 August.

Hinksey Yard was adapted as a 'virtual quarry', holding supplies of ballast for track renewal work. This was one of the few places where EWS employed a Class 08 shunter on a regular basis. On 14 May 2008 No. 08676 is shunting the yard as No. 66122 waits between duties.

Approaching Oxford station on 7 April 1990, No. 56022 returns north with empty coal wagons from Didcot Power Station.

Passing south through Oxford station on 30 August 2013 is yet another heavily laden Freightliner train for Southampton behind No. 66591. Mind you, they are probably mostly empty containers.

Passing southward through the platform road at Oxford on 17 August 1988 is No. 47079 with a return 'Binliner' on behalf of Avon County Council.

It's the 'Binliner' again, this time seen just north of Oxford and in the hands of No. 37715 *British Petroleum*. 31 May 1994.

In 1985 British Railways introduced a number of cross-London InterCity trains that stopped at Kensington Olympia. This station had latterly only seen limited local trains. The new trains continued south to locations including Brighton, Dover and Gatwick Airport. No. 47412 stops at the station on one such northbound train. Note that the station footbridge has been rebranded with the InterCity name.

The Blue Pullman was a short-lived venture to create a luxury train to rival the VSOE or Northern Belle stock. No. 47709 *Dionysus* passes through Olympia with the stock on 1 June 2006.

West Coast Railways Class 47 No. 47580 *County of Essex* hauls Black Five No. 44932 on a positioning move for a steam special excursion. The 47 is painted in the style in which Stratford TMD turned it out in 1977 to celebrate HM the Queen's Silver Jubilee.

When Eurostar services first started they operated out of Waterloo and the stock was serviced at North Pole Junction, Acton. Trains would pass through Kensington Olympia to and from the depot. To rescue failed trains, pairs of Class 73s were adapted with the special coupling gear needed. Nos 73118 and 73130 haul a Eurostar train back to the depot on 26 September 1996.

When BR closed the Southern Region lines west of Exeter, the remaining service to Waterloo was placed in the hands of Western Region Warship Class diesel-hydraulics. D823 *Hermes* awaits departure from Waterloo in 1969.

With the withdrawal of the hydraulics, Waterloo–Exeter services became worked by Class 50s. These services became included under Network SouthEast for operating convenience, although Exeter can hardly be called part of the South East! No. 50018 *Resolution* carries the original style of NSE livery as it passes through Clapham Junction on 3 August 1988.

Class 47s were also drafted in on these services. No. 47715 *Haymarket*, an ex-Scottish-based locomotive, passes through Clapham Junction towards the end of its journey on 11 March 1993.

Class 50 No. 50030 *Repulse* approaches Wimbledon on 27 August 1991. It is in the second style of Network SouthEast livery.

Class 33s were also used, mainly on the semi-fast stopping services to Salisbury. No. 33102 waits at Waterloo on 25 July 1987. The Class 33/1 variant was fitted with push-pull working with 4TC sets between Bournemouth and Weymouth as that section of line was not originally electrified.

In full NSE livery, and with matching stock, No. 33114 *Ashford 150* speeds through Raynes Park on 18 October 1992.

Another Class 33 on passenger, but this time No. 33063 has charge of the VSOE Pullman stock passing through Vauxhall on 12 September 1987.

No. 33048 pulls out of the carriage sidings at Clapham Junction with empty stock as 4VEP EMU No. 7827 enters the station on the Down fast line.

Motive power variety at Clapham Junction including No. 33046 *Merlin*. 14 August 1994.

Unusual visitors to the South Western Main Line as Class 20s Nos 20117 and 20121 work the 'Solent & Wessex Wanderer' railtour through Vauxhall on 1 March 1992. Class 33 No. 33116 is also included – probably to provide train heating.

The aftermath of another special at Vauxhall. Royal train-liveried Class 67 No. 67006 *Royal Sovereign* works the empty stock back to Clapham Junction on 21 June 2009.

Sunday engineering work is taking place near Weybridge on 24 June 2012 and EWS No. 66128 is in attendance, preventing trains from stopping at the London-bound platform.

On to the Windsor lines, and Fragonset-liveried No. 31452 *Minotaur* is bringing empty stock from the Mid-Hants Railway up to London for a 'Cathedrals Express' steam excursion. It is seen passing through Putney on 10 September 2003.

Near Barnes, No. 47736 *Cambridge Traction & Rolling Stock Depot* is bringing the VSOE Pullman stock towards Waterloo on 18 June 1996. This may have been for a special working in connection with racing at Ascot.

Freshly painted in EWS colours, No. 37406 *The Saltaire Society* brings a pair of barrier wagons through Barnes station on 21 May 2003.

Near Hounslow, West Coast Railways No. 47245 hauls a special train run in connection with Girlguiding UK. The train had been steam-hauled to Windsor and was one of a series of trips that ran on 3 May 2010.

EWS No. 66061 passes through Staines with an Eastleigh to Hoo Junction engineering works train in early 2013.

Approaching Staines from the London direction is Freightliner's No. 66555 with another engineering works train. 2 April 2013.

Back on the main line just south of Woking, Mainline-liveried No. 37798 is bringing an empty Mendip Rail stone train out of the stone terminal and back on to the running lines to return to Acton yard. A local train has been held at the signal while the 37 crosses ahead of it. 24 March 1995.

Guildford station has been completely rebuilt since this picture of No. 47622 was taken in January 1986.

Approaching Basingstoke is Hanson-liveried No. 59104 *Village of Great Elm*, seen passing stabled electric stock on 22 May 2001.

Into Basingstoke, and here cross-country passenger trains to Bournemouth and Poole come in via the line to Reading. Class 47 No. 47479 will take this route, reversing at Reading station before continuing northbound via Oxford. 26 September 1987.

Also on 26 September 1987, No. 33117 departs with a stopping train towards Salisbury formed of a 4TC push-pull set.

South Central Lines from Victoria

Gatwick Express was introduced on 12 May 1984 as a dedicated non-stop service between London Victoria and the airport. Previously a portion had been detached from Bognor Regis/Littlehampton EMU trains at the airport. Gatwick Express employed Class 73 locomotives with Mark 2 coaches and a driving trailer at the London end, converted from AC electric stock. On 30 May No. 73138 demonstrates the new order as it awaits departure in Victoria.

Gatwick Express proved successful and has continued in various guises ever since. On a wet 12 May 1986 No. 73123 *Gatwick Express* passes through Clapham Junction with a headboard to mark the second anniversary of the service.

It is 24 July 1997 and No. 73211 is approaching journey's end as it enters Horley with yet another Gatwick Express trip.

The Southern Region's Class 73 electro-diesels were versatile locomotives and maids of all work. They have carried a variety of liveries throughout their long lives. Repainted in original green livery as E6003 *Sir Herbert Walker*, this example is working a special excursion train through Brixton on 14 August 1994.

A Pathfinder railtour is the reason for this rare visit by Class 37 No. 37422 *Cardiff Canton* to the East Grinstead and Uckfield lines, here passing Riddlesdown on 2 February 2008.

Approaching Redhill station is No. 33042 on an aggregates train. 2 August 1989.

Class 33s No. 33030 and No. 33202 *The Burma Star* pass through Redhill station with a stone train on 16 April 1996.

Mainline-liveried No. 37248 *Midland Railway Centre* is stabled at Redhill with an engineering works train of new track panels. 4 April 1997.

More track replacement is forthcoming as No. 33118 brings track panels between Horley and Gatwick Airport, probably heading for the engineering sidings at Three Bridges.

Class 33s Nos 33051 *Shakespeare Cliff* and 33050 *Isle of Grain* head out of Brighton with a special train run in connection with an open day at the traction maintenance depot there on 22 September 1991.

British Railways' Southern Region introduced a batch of twenty-four DC electric locomotives in 1958 (later Class 71). They were fitted with an auxiliary pantograph for working in some sidings where overhead wires were installed for safety reasons. The pioneer of the class was retained by the National Railway Museum and in the 1990s was restored to working order for special trips. Here it is seen on an enthusiasts' special on 20 April 1996. The location is Hampden Park Junction, near Eastbourne, from where it is returning.

South London Line

An InterCity train passes through Wandsworth Road station on 21 November 1991 behind No. 47819. This will have stopped earlier at Kensington Olympia. The chimneys of Battersea Power Station can be seen sticking up above the locomotive.

Fast forward to February 2014 and a railtour passes through headed by DRS Class 20 No. 20303. Another of the class, No. 20304, is on the rear. This view is from the station footbridge, which gives an excellent panoramic view. Local services at this station now form part of the London Overground network and one of their trains has just departed for Clapham Junction.

The EWS Class 67s are often used on the VSOE (now Belmond) Pullman stock, and here No. 67002 is seen so employed, passing through Denmark Hill on 12 June 2009.

The South London Line is the route for cross-London freight trains to and from Kent. No. 58040 *Cottam Power Station* emerges from the tunnel and threads through Denmark Hill on 11 May 1997.

EWS-liveried No. 60012 has passed through Nunhead station and takes the road towards Lewisham with a return aggregates train. 11 October 1996.

South Eastern Lines from Charing Cross and Victoria

And now for something completely different! During the mid and late 1980s, London Underground's preserved electric locomotive, No. 12 *Sarah Siddons*, worked a few excursions over the Southern third rail tracks. On 21 September 1985 it hauled an excursion from Victoria to Folkestone West for passengers to visit the Romney, Hythe & Dymchurch Railway. It was pictured passing Beckenham Junction. The LT-style destination board reads 'New Romney via Folkestone West'.

Class 56 No. 56041 passes through Grove Park with ARC-liveried hopper wagons, returning from the ARC terminal at Chislehurst.

Sweeping along near Chislehurst, No. 92001 has a train of cargowaggons presumably bound for Dollands Moor and on through the Channel Tunnel. 16 August 1996.

The unique Pullman-liveried Class 73 No. 73101 *The Royal Alex* is appropriately matched with the VSOE Pullman coaches on a Valentine's Day excursion into Kent in 2001. It is passing through Shortlands and approaching Bromley South.

In 1999 the preserved Deltic D9000 *Royal Scots Grey* was hired for a summer season Saturdays train from Birmingham to Ramsgate. On 14 August the outward bound train is departing from Bromley South in typical Deltic fashion!

Yeoman-liveried No. 59004 *Paul A. Hammond* passes Petts Wood Junction on 12 September 2001. The long footbridge here, popular since steam days, was later meshed in.

EWS Class 66 No. 66036 nears Swanley with a train of Cargowagons on 15 August 2001.

At Otford Junction, near Sevenoaks, Freightliner Class 66 No. 66612 hauls a train of Railtrack self-unloading ballast wagons that are new at this time. 19 June 2002.

Class 73 No. 73106 enters Paddock Wood while hauling an EMU that appears to have suffered accident damage. 8 February 1992.

Entering Ashford, Nos 33116 (D6535) *Hertfordshire Railtours* and 73119 *Kentish Mercury* top-and-tail a pair of inspection saloons. The building of HS1 has completely changed the view at this location, while Ashford station itself has been rebuilt and now carries the grander name of Ashford International. 14 July 1994.

On the north side of Kent, skirting the River Thames, Colas Class 70 No. 70806 passes through Stone Crossing with an Eastleigh–Hoo Junction working on 11 June 2014. The level crossing that gave the station its name, seen at the loco end of the platform, has since been closed to traffic and replaced by a new pedestrian and cycle footbridge.

On 15 June 2017 the same train is in the hands of Colas No. 66846 as it passes through Northfleet. The platforms here are staggered.

Seen between Northfleet and Gravesend, on this occasion the Eastleigh to Hoo Junction engineering works train has a consignment of rails and is hauled by No. 66848. 7 July 2015.

The Network Rail track inspection train has visited Gravesend with a pair of DRS Class 37s providing the motive power. No. 37606 is at the western end. 2 June 2007.

EWS No. 66074 enters Gravesend station with a train of MRL box wagons on 10 April 2017.

There is snow on the ground as No. 66137 passes through Gravesend with more wagons for Hoo Junction. 12 March 2013.

Entering Gravesend station from the west and taking the centre road is EWS No. 66007 with a loaded train of open bogie wagons. 9 July 2013.

Direct Rail Services Class 66 No. 66303 passes through Gravesend with a container train for Thamesport. Over the Christmas of 2013, Gravesend station was rebuilt with the two centre roads being replaced by another platform road for westbound trains. The London-bound platform on the left then became a terminating bay.

The new layout at Gravesend. A dedicated Class 31 with the Network Rail track inspection train passes through Platform 2. The new Platform 1 occupies the site of the former Up through road, while the left-hand platform, now a bay, is numbered zero. 26 June 2014.

Acknowledgements and Bibliography

Beer, Brian, *Diesels in the Capital* (Sparkford: Oxford Publishing Co., 1990).

Kennedy, Rex, *Ian Allan's 50 Years of Railways 1942-1992* (London: BCA, 1992).

Rawlinson, Mark, *Freightmaster: The National Railfreight Guide* (Swindon: Freightmaster Publishing, various editions).

Rawlinson, Mark, *British Railways Pocket Book No. 1: Locomotives* (Sheffield: Platform 5 Publishing, various editions).